DISCOVER
TO
RECOVER

Cover design by: Emergence Publishers

Library of Congress Control Number: 2018675309

Printed in the United States of America

DEDICATION

This book is dedicated to God Almighty, the fountain of wisdom.

TABLE OF CONTENTS

PREFACE

The purpose of a thing is more than the capacity of that thing. Such a weird opening. Don't you think?

But really, think about it. If the purpose of a car is the capacity of the car, what do you think speed will do to people driving cars?

The purpose of anything is more about functionality than capacity. Let's put it in proper perspective, the purpose of a thing is about HOW you put the CAPACITY of that thing to FUNCTION.

On February 22, 2019, Robert Sylvester Kelly, an American former singer and songwriter, was apprehended, after several court hearings, he was sentenced to prison for multiple counts of charges of sex trafficking, sex exploitation of minors, producing child pornography, etc.

While already serving a 30-year prison sentence, for sex trafficking, in February 2023, he got another 20-year sentence for child porn (CNN February 23, 2023.)

What do you think of this?

Truth be told, R. Kelly is talented and has a profound gift with music. When it comes to music, he does it very well. R. Kelly has been credited with prolific successes in both R&B and hip hop, according to the New York Times, he earned nicknames such as "the King of R&B", "the King of Pop-Soul", and the "Pied Piper of R&B."

He recorded 18 studio albums and sold over 75 million albums and singles worldwide. He received 3 Grammy awards in 1998 and other several awards including being featured in the Guinness World Records.

His record is legendary.

But what is he doing in incarceration?

What happened to this "legend?"

We can go on and on to attempt to note his crimes. We can attempt also to dig up atrocities he committed that never surfaced in the media. Would we be correct to say these things and maybe more were the reasons why he is in prison?

The answer is no.

Seeing the fact that he is in prison, "Justice has been served," many would say.

Many deals were canceled, and several online streaming channels removed his account and content from their platforms. Some people would say "Karma finally caught up with him."

I want you to look at the big picture. If you do, you will see that this conversation is not about R. Kelly, neither is this book.

Hang on, let's delve deeper into what this conversation is about.

Part One:

Illusions of Freedom

CHAPTER ONE

PURPOSE OF LIFE

You would not be surprised to hear that the purpose of life is more than living. But how? We have established that capacity and functionality are not the same. You're alive, it means you can express the features and characteristics of living things. It also means you're living. However, the purpose of your life is more than your living. This implies that there's so much that we cannot sweep under the carpet about HOW we live. Remember our last conversation? The purpose of life is not in the ability to demonstrate that you're a living being and also a human. In essence, it is not in having the capacity or characteristics you have rather it is in HOW this capacity or characteristics is put to function.

People live their lives without a how. In other words, people are giving expression to their living capacity without a HOW (a map, a guide, or an instruction manual). This is why we have a rampant case of dysfunctional individuals and families. This is because they are running their individual lives and their family lives with a HOW they understand.

What does this mean?

HOW, in this conversation, means a method or methodology. HOW is a guide. HOW is an instruction manual. It won't be surprising that this is not news to you but here's the catch:

HOW is the fruit of a WHY.

What this means is that your method or methodology, map, guide, or instruction, must stem from a revelation of the reason why it is designed, given, or adopted.

Let me leave you with a question.

On what method, methodology, guide, map, or instruction is your life or family running?

There's life and there's style.

The purpose of life is WHY the life is given, this WHY determines the choice of style that forms a person's or family's lifestyle. On the whole, we don't measure our individual lives and family lives based on our capacity (what we can do) but on functionality (how it operates and why it operates in that certain way).

But today, we do not see the world functioning as it should because of dysfunction. People are living lives that aren't theirs as they copy the fancy of other people's lives seeing that they have failed to establish their authentic self and their style (how and why).

Families envy the bliss they see in other families and are trying to function like them without having and establishing an appreciable knowledge of the value systems of those families.

This is why we must journey into understanding the depth of dysfunction besetting individuals, families, and society. It is the foundation for truly appreciating the knowledge of purpose.

In Genesis 1:28, God said, "Let them have dominion over the fish of the seas, birds of the air...." The general idea of purpose is entrenched in dominion over the earth. This purpose is twofold: all-time dominion by all men; and per-time mandate for each man.

In essence, God created the earth as an extension of His Kingdom (Heaven's colony) and put man as its ambassador. We cannot leave the fact that there's a Governor who communicates the values of the Kingdom in the colony and supervises that the intent of the Supreme Lord is carried out. This Governor is the Holy Spirit.

The first layer of purpose is the ability given to man to freely exercise dominion. Being born on the earth and sharing in the characteristics of humans qualifies for this dominion. The second layer of purpose is a mandate for the recreated man. Being born again by the washing of the water and blood qualifies for sharing in this mandate. God has revealed the all-time purpose but He communicates his intent (mandate per time) through His Spirit in the hearts of the recreated humans.

While the conversation on purpose will be continued in part two of this book, it is important to state assertively that every man, from birth, received the gift of free will. Every human begins to express free will from the age of consciousness. Let's deepen this conversation on freedom.

CHAPTER TWO

TEST OF FREEDOM

There is an article "What Does Freedom Mean?" written by Dr. Sean McDowell in 2021 that captured an interview conducted among a set of students in high school. Unanimously, the student agreed on a definition: "Freedom is being able to do what you want without restraint."

Look at this definition. How else can the definition of freedom be rendered?

Let's break it a little bit.

This means doing whatever he or she wants without any person or law standing in their way. You agree with this, don't you?

In other words, our pursuits as humans are engendered in our desire to find the freedom that allows us to express our innermost self in the way we want.

What most people don't know is that there is a difference between what a free person does and what a person does freely.

Now I want to ask you a question. Is the person who does what he or she wants really free? Think about it.

Now the definition above tells you that freedom refers to what a person (free or not) does freely but there is a difference between the person's status and the person's action. We will buttress this as continue.

If what we do defines our freedom status, then in doing what we do, we can become more free. Are we more free when we drink 6 glasses of water because we're thirsty? Would you eat every single food on the table during a dinner party simply because every meal on the table is sumptuous and good-looking?

The person who does what he or she wants is not truly free. Your freedom is you not what you do. According to McDowell, "True freedom is not a matter of doing what you want without restraint, but cultivating the right wants and living in obedience to God's will."

Your emotions and wants are not your master. If you let your emotions and desires become your master and lead you, they will turn you into a monster. In order not to let this happen, you must assert yourself as the master. In other words, freedom is established when your wants align with God's will. The reason why you plunge into God's will is simple: you do not know for sure what you want for yourself (your will) and you also do not know what the result of that will will be. The will of God for you is plain and simple "to give peace [wholeness, prosperity, completeness, harmony, tranquility] and hope and a posterity to you."

Think about it for a moment.

It is safe to plunge into God's will for you.

Again, if freedom means doing what you want without restraint, you would destroy yourself without even knowing.

Freedom is not about the absence of restraint.

Would you eat anything without restraint because it is how you feel?

Would you stay in bed all day because you don't feel like getting out of bed?

Would you keep eating because you don't feel like stopping even when you have had your fill?

Would you have sex with anyone and everyone because you feel like it?

That's not freedom. Sounds like bondage to me. This kind of freedom creates a situation I call freedom of bondage.

CHAPTER THREE

FREEDOM OF BONDAGE

Have you ever caught yourself not having an appetite for food at all? I think you have. Should you not eat for as long as you don't feel like eating? You know what not eating can do to anyone. Soon, you will lose strength and become weak. Soon you will die.

Assuming you are a foodie who has never had a 'no-appetite' experience, I will provide another example for you.

What causes weight gain? Does weight gain offer any health risks? So, if you love food, does that license you to eat and keep eating without a stop? Or does it imply you should anything edible anytime you find one?

When we look at the subject of freedom with a single glance, we want to make a subconscious assumption that it is a break from bondage or a response to every form of restraint. The true test of freedom is not in your ability to do everything you feel like doing or do nothing because you don't feel like doing anything.

When the Supreme Court announced its ruling to legalize same-sex marriage in America, President Barack Obama said "We are all more free." Because of "this victory," the White House was bathed in rainbow-colored light in celebration of that development. If you look closely at Obama's claim, you'd see a definition of "freedom" that many Americans will embrace without any regard to what they hold true about freedom.

Freedom, according to that definition, is inversely presented. Were Americans enslaved or in bondage in America before its Supreme Court's ruling? If yes, how exactly did the court's decision bequeath freedom to Americans? Note, Obama said it bequeathed more freedom to the pocket of Americans who felt they were in bondage because of the restraint to express their choice to legally be in same-sex marriage.

Who is more free? What metrics should be used to measure this?

None's more free. There are only those who are free and those who are in bonds. It's either one or the other.

This breed of people who claim to be more free are in a state of dysfunction.

Why does the Bugatti have brakes? I thought one of the most profound features the car has is speed. It is arguably reckoned as the fastest car in the world. Think about it again, why does the car have brakes?

So, when someone who's in bond, whose primary concern should be freedom, seeks to be more free, it results in what I call freedom of bondage. Let me explain this further.

If you don't need freedom, it is a sign you're not in bond. Only people in bond seek freedom. The thicker and stronger the bonds, the more free they should seek to become. That's how cars are designed too. Yes, the faster the ability the car has to run, the more effective speed brakes are required. It's a dysfunction for a speed car to have less effective speed brakes.

This is simply what President Obama said - set the beast free.

There can never be an anchor of dysfunction than this.

This is why freedom, according to these sources, implies the absence of as many restrictions as reasonably possible upon people's choices in life. Think about the effect of this. On the whole, it creates a situation I call freedom of bondage. It's going to engender dysfunction. Let's talk about this dysfunction in the next chapter.

Part Two:
True Freedom

CHAPTER FOUR

DYSFUNCTION

It is vital to understand that man has an inconceivable level of ability. Anything a man sets his mind to do, man will. This is why there's a need for a guide or an instruction manual to help a man become temperate in whatever the man chooses to do.

Without temperance, think about it for a second and imagine what a man will do.

If you are at least 40 years of age, have you ever imagined that a time will come, that someday, and that time is even now, that a human being will decide to choose to switch his or her gender status?

How does a man develop feelings for an animal (pet) so much so that he or she decides to get wedded to that animal and call it freedom?

If you allow yourself to do anything and everything you wish to do without any form of restraint or moderation, you will destroy yourself eventually. The entire pursuit of mankind is a journey to experiencing the freedom they already have and not the freedom they are searching for. Without moderation, the freedom mankind searches for and pursues becomes self-destructive. How else can we define self-mutiny if not this pursuit of dysfunctional desires mankind has embarked on?

The term dysfunction refers to an impairment, disturbance, or deficiency and may manifest in different ways and patterns in communication, emotions, relationships, behavior, etc.

The term dysfunctional has been widely used to describe unhealthy patterns and behavioral and relational dynamics. According to Laura Harold, "The term can feel stigmatizing. Because of this, some trauma-informed therapists suggest referring to these behaviors, patterns, and dynamics as unhealthy rather than dysfunctional." In any case, all dysfunctional patterns are unhealthy.

Without any form of restraint, unhealthy compulsive behaviors are given expression in various forms like gambling and alcoholism. It will allow for emotional, physical, and sexually abusive behaviors. It may allow for strange desires like sexual preference for minors that result in the sexual exploitation of minors. How about what has now become the LGBTQ movement or the community? In the past, all LGBTQ behaviors were considered as pervasive. The people were regarded as perverts. Today, we talk about inclusion and we are creating platforms to allow their behaviors to be expressed like any fundamental human right.

It doesn't matter what we call it today. What is unhealthy is unhealthy. Every attempt and effort to normalize what is unhealthy will exacerbate these dysfunctional behaviors. Without any form of restraint or restriction, the freedom people would embrace and pursue become self-destructive.

Self-determination or inclusion will not provide the solution. They are only a cry to allow people to become "more free" in doing what they want and however they want it. This creates a situation that absents the particular realities that restrict people from discovering themselves and becoming who they are and from fulfilling the identity given to them by God in creation so that they can be restored to that identity in redemption, and the corresponding liberty to choose only what reflects their true identity.

CHAPTER FIVE

DIFFERENCE VERSUS ODD

Our unique abilities are meant to be our difference and to serve as our authentic advantage on Earth. What this means is that, as a person, I should be able to find certain abilities or features that make me feel different, and see and understand myself differently. This difference, because it's my advantage, should be celebrated.

Are there situations where we find certain unique abilities or features that flaw our self-esteem? There could be and we would look into them. However, you must understand that everything has a purpose. Let me tell you a story.

A certain Master was passing by a city in the group of his students and they saw a blind man by the roadside. The story has it that this man was born blind. It means he'd never had the opportunity to see. He has never seen the sun. He'd never seen anything. He doesn't have an idea what his mother looks like.

Amidst a feeling of compassion and curiosity, one of the students summed up courage to ask the Master: who sinned? is it the man or his parent to warrant him born blind?

In those days, Masters were revered and believed to have vast knowledge.

The Master answered. You'd be shocked by what he said.

He said neither the man nor his parent sinned. So, why was he born blind? There was a purpose he was born blind. What's the purpose? "That the works of God will be made manifest in him." (John 9:14).

The students believed the reason why the man was born blind must be some sort of punishment for what he or the parents did. In other words, it could be some sort of course they incurred for one rebellious act or the other. The Master, on the other hand, knows that the man was born blind for a greater cause. That people will see and hear about the works of God through the man.

Another story:

There is a 41-year-old man who is married to a tall beautiful American-Japanese model whom he married in 2012 after he proposed to her on a yacht cruise. Together, they both have two sons and two daughters and they live in Southern California. The man is estimated to have a net worth of $5 million. He has given speeches to more than 3 million people across 60 countries.

His name is Nick Vujicic. Yes, the same Nick who was born without arms and legs. Think about it for a moment. "...without arms and legs." Let's rewind, he is married to a model?!

How?

If you were a lady, would you love a man without arms and legs, let alone marry him? Would you even agree to go on a date with him?

The life of Nick is a summary of what that Master taught His students: Nick was born the way he was so that the works of God can be made manifest.

Today, Nick has a ministry that champions the cause of the brokenhearted where he shares the gospel of Jesus Christ in various areas including prison ministry, youth ministry, etc.

Have you read the story of Lizzy Velasquez? I think you should. She is reckoned to be the ugliest woman in the world. Be that as it may, the works of God are made manifest through her.

Now, let's look at a most recent phenomenon - gender dysphoria, which differs from unique abilities that flaw our self-esteem. Today, every talk on gender dysphoria arguably engenders from identity crisis.

According to Geralyn Dexter, 'gender identity refers to the human sense of who they are and how they see and describe themselves.' Did you note "how they see and describe themselves?"

In the face of overwhelming evidence proving who they are, should 'how they see and (choose to) describe themselves' be given more recognition and considered more relevant than who they are from birth?

What happens to the facts?

From creation, every human created and born identifies as either "male" or "female". We know how to identify any human and every animal based on the features that stand them out as either male or female. Even a male mosquito is different from a female mosquito and this identity has nothing to do with what the male mosquito feels about himself. How the rat or rabbit sees and describes itself is not what should determine its gender, it already has a gender and we know for a fact that the rat or rabbit can be identified based on its genitals and other features that distinctively define it as either male or female.

On the contrary, some people feel their gender identity is different from their biological sex. This suggests that gender identity is making an effort to trump biological sex. For example, some people have male genitals and facial hair but do not identify as male or feel masculine and hence identify with a gender identity that they see and feel of themselves and describe themselves.

In the same manner, some people have female genitals and breasts but do not identify as female or feel feminine. Therefore, they have concluded that the concept of biological sex or gender is not relevant to their identity.

What can be more erroneous than this 'freedom of bondage?'

While this is what has come to be referred to as gender dysphoria, it needs to be painted in black and white. Let's call a spade a spade.

Gender dysphoria is gender identity.

Simply put, people suffering from gender dysphoria are bound to a crisis of identity. We already know what gender identity means, before we say what crisis of identity means, let's find a definition for gender dysphoria.

It is a feeling of unease that a person may have because of a mismatch between their biological sex and their gender identity.

Mismatch?

How do you know this?

An identity crisis is characterized by a period when a person's life is beset with confusion and uncertainty about their identity because their sense (perception) of identity is unstable and insecure.

Let me buttress that when a person (a man who has male genitals and facial hair) does not feel masculine is a normal feeling. Also, when a woman who has female genitals and breasts does not feel feminine, that feeling is normal. Let me tell you what is not normal.

The assertion is that having these biological features that typically identify a person as either a male or female is not relevant to that person's identity. If these biological features are not relevant, what then is?

Feelings?

How do you have a wall painted in white and call it black simply because you feel different about the color?

What you think or how you feel is inconsequential but not irrelevant. In this book, there is one thing that needs to be emphasized. It is the insecurity that comes with how people see themselves and what people because of how they see themselves.

How do you see yourself?

What do you think about yourself?

To answer this question, you must have a revelation of:

1. Who you are?

2. ☐Whose you are?

3. ☐ What you have?

We will talk about these.

CHAPTER SIX

CRISES OF IDENTITY

It is identity crises that make people seek external validation in making odd decisions rather than appreciating their differences. Every decision is a product of choice. In this case, it is a choice between alternatives: difference or odd.

Choice is a gift

There is a statement I once that changed my entire life. "We make our choices and then our choices make us." It is such a simple sentence yet, it is so powerful.

I will tell you a story.

The relationship between Lauren and her parent has been soured in the last 9 months. Each time she returns from school, she goes upstairs and locks herself up in her room all day. It started when her parent found out that 15-year-old Lauren had gotten herself a boyfriend in school. When the dad confronted her, he instructed her to cut all ties and end her relationship with her boyfriend but she reacted threatening to run away with the boy if her parent won't let them be.

Wait...

This is certainly not the first time you have heard a story like this one. Of course not.

Nut why am I telling you this one? I want us to look into the reasons why this story keeps replaying itself in different homes and families.

What happens when kids don't learn to find validation from within?

I mean when kids don't get to accept themselves for who they are.

I mean when kids don't get to love themselves based on their uniqueness.

I mean when kids don't get to be fulfilled with who they have come to know themselves to be.

It starts with them knowing who they are, whose they are, and what they have. Remember, I said we would talk about this.

Lauren was ready to defy her dad and leave with her boyfriend. Why?

Before we look into why, let's briefly scour through the possible implications of making such a choice.

Probably;

She would drop out of school.

She may not get to go to college.

She may become a teenage mum.

She might lose her relationship with her parent.

All these for a boy? No.

It is a crisis of identity.

Only the boy makes her feel the way only she can explain. That feeling comes from the validation she gets from him.

He compliments her. He tells her she is beautiful. He tells her she is smart. He tells her she is brave.

So, Lauren only feels good when she is with her boyfriend. She didn't find validation from within herself and she also didn't find it from within her home from her parent. She found it from someone outside. Her parent never told her she was beautiful, smart, or brave.

Because of how good the boy makes her feel about herself, she can do the unthinkable in response, including defying her father's instruction. Now, she wears the kind of apparel that makes him give her more compliments. She wants to walk the way he wants her to so he can give her compliments.

I heard a man share a story and I learned a very profound lesson. He said his little daughter made a drawing of him and brought it to him to see. When he saw it, he didn't say "This is beautiful, I love it. I am proud of you."

If you were a father, what would you say when your daughter makes a drawing of you and brings it to you?

"You are such a genius!" you would say, I am guessing.

But this man didn't say anything like that.

Rather he said to her, "After you drew it, how did you feel?"

It's a hard question but he had a reason for asking.

He wanted her to pause and look inward and find the real feeling and authentic fulfillment that comes with starting a task and completing it, for putting her creative ability to use and the feeling of having her father's image replicated on paper by her. When she looks inward to find this feeling, it would matter MORE than the external validation she sought from her dad. This way, she would learn to find validation from within. It is best.

Lauren didn't get to learn to garner validation from within. Her parent didn't know better enough to teach her as well as to help her find validation from within the family.

Today, a lot of people are not different from Lauren because they have a similar desire to find validation in the wrong places.

Let's talk about the use of apparel, for example.

With a single glance, today, we can conclude that the purpose of apparel has a clear-cut difference with fashion. The idea of fashion is now sandwiched with trends, styles, preferences, and everything that is about personal appearance that makes people happy.

Did you note "personal appearance that makes people happy?"

We understand that apparel is for covering. No doubt about this. Fashion on the other hand is introduced as an alteration of the purpose and intention behind the use of apparel. As it pertains to physical appearance, the introduction of fashion is the point where the concept of human esteem begins to become tampered with while being camouflaged as its fix.

What do I mean?

Today, people have clothes in their wardrobes that make them feel good and confident about themselves.

Think about it for a moment.

A person's confidence and self-esteem stemming from a garment? The same garment will be passed into the bin. Another garment is implored again as the source of confidence. Is this a joke?

Can this really be the fix?

No. It's a camouflage. It's a facade.

Today, if someone passes a backhanded compliment to a lady because of the garment she is wearing, she will likely never wear that garment again.

Pause for a moment and think about it.

Do we wear what we wear because of us or because of people?

Put another way:

When we wear apparel, is it the design that matters most or the person who is wearing the apparel?

We see this everywhere. People do things because of what people have said or what they long for people to say. There is a crisis of identity.

From what we have seen and learned about gender dysphoria, we can assert that many people with gender dysphoria have a desire to live a life that "matches" or expresses their gender identity instead of accepting their biological sex.

This, they do by changing the way they look and behave.

Some people with gender dysphoria, but not all, may want to use hormones and sometimes go for surgery to express their gender identity. Can you pause for a moment to think about this?

Let's talk:

So, what does expressing gender identity mean?

Very simple.

It means defying their biological gender.

It means asserting how they see themselves and what they choose to describe themselves based on the way they see themselves. Sometimes, they go as far as undergoing gender reassignment surgery.

What are the possible implications of transgender and reassigned gender on human identity?

There would be a disconnect with one's original and authentic self.

There could be health complications like Injury to the urinary tract, hematoma, nerve injury, etc.

According to Richard P. Fitzgibbons, sexual reassignment surgery and transgender issues pose a risk of psychiatric disorders like depression, anxiety disorder, suicidal ideation, suicide attempts, self-harm without lethal intent, etc. More concisely, he said

"...persons after sex reassignment, have considerably higher risks for mortality, suicidal behavior, and psychiatric morbidity than the general population.... Most shockingly, their suicide mortality rose almost to 20-fold above the comparable non-transgender population."

This is not different from Lauren.

The presence of Lauren's boyfriend appears to be the solution to her lack of validation. A closer look has shown us that this solution does not address the root cause of the problem. Just seeking a sense of confidence from the attire you wear is a façade. It does not solve the root cause of the deficiency of feeling confident. Hormonal affirming treatment and gender reassignment surgery CANNOT address the root cause of gender dysphoria. Funny how advocates of transgender emphasize that gender dysphoria is not a medical condition yet they implore medical procedures for people living with gender dysphoria.

This is a self-inflicted bondage.

Part Three:

Discovery and Recovery

CHAPTER SEVEN

TRUE IDENTITY

One of the things a lot of people don't get to be taught early in their lives is the secret of discovering their true identity. Let me buttress this: you are a reflection of your Source.

Who's your source?

"Earnestly remember your Creator before the silver cord [of life] is broken, or the golden bowl is crushed, or the pitcher at the fountain is shattered and the wheel at the cistern is crushed; 7 then the dust [out of which God made man's body] will return to the earth as it was, and the spirit will return to God who gave it."

Ecclesiastes 12:6-7

It is clear that there is a God who created the earth and everything in it and He is the fountain from which everything finds expression. If you believe in the existence of God, you should also accept the message of the Bible. Categorically, the Bible tells us in Genesis 1, that we were created by God. Yes, we were created by using the dust of the ground. The Bible didn't stop there. It shows us how. God used the dust of the ground to give us a frame and a body but He shared Himself (His breath) with us. Therefore, God is our source.

We, therefore, do not have an identity outside our Source. Iteratively, we are a reflection of our Source.

What is a reflection?

According to Dictionary.com, reflection refers to "casting back a light or heat, mirroring, or giving back or showing an image." In other words, when we function as a reflection of our Source, we cast back, mirror, and (or) show God forth.

It is this simple.

Any identity sought anywhere outside our source will be met with great resistance from creation. The word that closely describes every effort to find an identity outside God - the Source of everything, is pervasion.

Let's further our discussion on identity.

Seeing that we have established that we are created to reflect God as a means to finding and expressing our identity, we can reflect a God that we know. This means that how much of God we know is proportionate to the level of the identity we can express. In any case, one cannot find his or her true identity outside God.

The most audacious words you would find in the Bible are those that are written in red letters and they were spoken by Jesus. One of such words is found in John 15.

"I am the true Vine, and My Father is the vinedresser. Every branch in Me that does not bear fruit, He takes away; and every branch that continues to bear fruit, He [repeatedly] prunes, so that it will bear more fruit [even richer and finer fruit]. You are already clean because of the word which I have given you [the teachings which I have discussed with you]." John□ 15□:1□-3□ AMP

Did you see your identity in these words of Jesus? I am sure you did.

Wait until I show you what He further said. He went on to advise us:

"Remain in Me, and I [will remain] in you. Just as no branch can bear fruit by itself without remaining in the vine, neither can you [bear fruit, producing evidence of your faith] unless you remain in Me." John□ 15□:4□ AMP□□□□□□□□□□

Jesus didn't just advise us. He told us WHY He advised us. WE CANNOT BEAR FRUIT UNLESS WE REMAIN IN THE VINE (Jesus).

We already know from the Bible (Hebrews 1:3) that Jesus is the express image of God. Everything we know of God is found in the expression of the deity and the person of Jesus. This is why only He could tell us He is the Vine and we can do NOTHING except we are in Him. □□□□□

Here's where it gets complicated, how true is the statement that those who are not in Him (the Vine) can do nothing?

Going by what you see, you would assume that there are a lot of people who do not know God, hence, they are not in the Vine, but they are doing something. The word 'something' refers to something that is going on for them.

To comment on this, let me digress a little.

In Matthew 28:18, "Jesus said all power in heaven and on earth has been given to me." [New Century Version].

Somewhere in Africa, whether the climate is due for rain or not, one man can make incantations and rain will begin to fall.

But how?

Didn't Jesus say all power has been given to Him? What power are these rainmakers using?

They are perverts who fraternize with spirits and manipulate the elements to make rain fall. Simply put, these people are assisted because, in themselves, they do not have any power. Therefore, they enter into partnership with other perverts (demon spirits) who are already condemned but awaiting punishment. It is this participatory act required in partnership agreements that make them perverts too.

In essence, you can really DO NOTHING when you're not in the Vine. You can DO EVERYTHING when you're in the Vine. With God (in the Vine), all things are possible (Matthew 19:26). You have everything to gain being in the Vine. You have lost everything outside the Vine.

When you're in the Vine, it is easy to live a life that reflects God and to participate in carrying out His will. How do you become a branch and share in Vine?

Submit your life to the leadership of Jesus.

Confess your sin, renounce every right over your will, and ask Jesus to come into your life.

CHAPTER EIGHT

YOU DON'T HAVE A PURPOSE

In the previous chapter, we have learned that when it pertains to the subject of our identity, our work is capsuled in one word: reflect God. After this, we must come to this knowing that God has a will for the Earth, and within this will, our work is also capsuled in a single word: represent Him.

How do we represent God?

Do His will.

Sounds absurd?

It is not. It is just what it is. No one can do the will of God without being in the Vine. Remember, the Bible said God, by Himself, dresses the Vine (John 15:1).

What does Vinedresser mean?

It refers to the One who prunes: grow and nurture and cultivate. A part of pruning involves removing diseased or dead plants. So, Jesus said every branch in Him (the Vine) that does not bear fruits He (the Vinedresser) takes away.

In the previous chapter, Jesus said without your being in the Vine, you can do nothing but you should understand the other part of the message, being in the Vine enables you to bear much fruit. The word enable here refers to grace, without which, according to Jesus, you would do nothing. Do nothing here means bear no fruits and by implication, withers and dies and the consequence of this is that they are gathered and thrown into the fire and they burn.

John 15:6

This is principally the meaning of purpose: bearing much fruits.

Time and time again, you hear people say they are in search of their purpose. I believe you have heard such too. You probably have said so, too. Listen, there's no such thing as your purpose or my purpose. There's only God's purpose. This is why people pray and seek to find purpose and never find it when in reality, what they seek is not purpose.

Let's demonstrate this.

When a teacher assigns his students to perform a task or to do something else, it is not the student's responsibility to know why the teacher has asked them to perform that task. For example, a teacher can give homework to his students. The students don't know why and it should not be a thing of concern to the students. Theirs is to do what has been assigned to them. The purpose of the homework may be to familiarize themselves with the next topic in the curriculum or maybe the teacher wants the students to get a deeper understanding of the last topic he taught them.

Now can you see how and why I said there's no such thing as finding or seeking purpose?

The purpose is God's.

This we can understand better when we consider the creation story in the Bible. In the beginning, God (Elohim)created the heavens and the earth (Genesis 1:1). There's no doubt about this. Like the book title of Simon Sinek, Start with Why is a natural order. The Bible specifically tells us why God created the earth and everything in it saying "Let them (man) have dominion (over the living creature) made by God for man.

CHAPTER NINE

YOUR TRUE POTENTIAL

Purpose is not such a hard thing to understand. I believe you know this now. God, having a will (purpose) for the earth, placed man to represent Him to do such will. This is where the concept of potential suffices.

Think about it for a second. What enables a man to do God's will? Potential.

Most simply and naturally possible, potential can be explained to mean what can be that is yet to be. In essence, what you can do that you are yet to do, what you can become that you're yet to become, and what you can have that you're yet to have.

When you look closely at what has been noted above, you will see that what potential means is latent power. Latent power, simply put, means abilities that exist in hidden and dormant form.

Beyond seeing power from the latent perspective of dormant abilities, we can move further into understanding this concept as an enabler.

It is good that we have established that potential is power. Now, let's reference the meaning of power from the Bible in Acts of the Apostles.

"how God anointed Jesus of Nazareth with the Holy Spirit and with power, who went about doing good... for God was with Him."

"But you shall receive power when the Holy Spirit has come upon you; and you shall be witnesses to Me..."

The process is simple: the Holy Ghost comes in first and then power comes next. There's nobody who bore much fruits in the Bible without this enabler, the Holy Ghost. Another example is when the angel - Gabriel visited Mary with the news of the virgin birth, "Then Mary said to the angel, "How can this be, since I do not know a man?" And the angel answered and said to her, "The Holy Spirit will come upon you, and the power of the Highest will overshadow you..." Luke□ 1□:34□-35□ NKJV

□Potential is the power resident in us that enables us to do what we cannot do on our own: do good, be witnesses of Jesus, and bear much fruits.

Take a second and ponder on this:

"For we are His workmanship [His own master work, a work of art], created in Christ Jesus [reborn from above—spiritually transformed, renewed, ready to be used] for good works, which God prepared [for us] beforehand [taking paths which He set], so that we would walk in them [living the good life which He

prearranged and made ready for us].
Ephesians□ 2□:10□ AMP

□□□□□□□□□□□□□□

CHAPTER TEN

YOUR WORK TOOLS

Gifts are tools. When it comes to performing a task or carrying out an assignment, certain tools will be required for such performance.

Knowing that God creates humans with a purpose, God also knows what they would need to get that job done. In other words, a man needs certain tool(s) to do God's purpose - his assignment.

According to Brittany Yesudasan, "God is the most generous gift-giver you can ever know."

Isn't this amazing?

Let me tell you what is even more amazing. Seeing that God's purpose, your assignment, means doing His will, He decided to give to those who accept to abide in Him (through Jesus) the gift of Himself.

Aside from this, God also gives individuals unique gifts. This is because everyone is on a unique spiritual journey with God. One thing we know is that God never changes but how He expresses Himself through humanity differs.

This is to buttress the knowing that God has a purpose and He also has a plan for everyone's life. This plan plays a specific part in His master plan.

God's overarching plan is that, through the lives of people and the expression of His abilities in them, He would be magnified and made known in the world.

gifts are different from talents. Talents are specific abilities we can liken to skills. It is just like the skill one possesses at the piano or in a sport. Talents are abilities that come from practice and development through hard work. People who do not have the gift of God's presence (Holy Spirit) within them still have many talents, but oftentimes, they do not give expression to bearing much fruits.

If you abide in the Vine (Jesus), finding your gifts becomes clearer, and putting this gift to use becomes easier.

CHAPTER ELEVEN

THRIVING ENVIRONMENT

Personality, simply put, means a way of thinking, feeling, and behaving. It embraces attitudes, moods, and opinions that create the necessary environment that enables your assignment to be executed.

In other words, the environment that makes it favorable for your gift to thrive, as well as your potential, depends so much on the way you think, feel, and generally behave. Therefore, your assignment will flourish proportionately with your personality.

Personality ensures a consistent difference that exists between people and this is why and how God deals uniquely and differently with people whom He bestows assignments on.

You're different. God's assignment for you is uniquely different. Your attitude, mood, and opinion is a response and it must be uniquely different. This is how you maintain the environment that allows your assignment to thrive. When we do this, we assert our participatory contribution to God's purpose of making His Kingdom come.

CHAPTER TWELVE

THE REAL STAYING POWER

When it comes to the word passion, many people do not know the meaning of the word as they use it interchangeably with gifts. In contemporary literature and round table discussions, you hear things like 'profiting from your passion' or 'turning your passion to profit.'

Until now, I'm in awe of what they mean. This is because passion, if understood, does not fit the context of such discussions.

What then is passion?

I will simplify it in a way you will understand.

What makes a farmer return to his farm after a year of port harvest?

Passion for farming.

What makes an evangelist leave the comfort of his home and go out into the streets or into the villages to tell people about Jesus?

Passion for dying souls.

What takes people away from their country into new countries for missions, despite persecution and other threats to their lives, to share the goodness of Jesus?

Passion for God's desire that ALL men be saved.

There's low church attendance, but despite that, the pastor keeps the church door open and preaches his heart out every church service day. Why?

Passion for his assignment.

Now, this is passion. In other words, passion is grace.

How else can we understand it? It is the seed of an insatiable desire to fulfill a God-given assignment despite the challenges, setbacks, and limitations. The Bible says, in Philippians 2:13, that it is God who works in us both to will and to do for His good pleasure.

You probably have seen why I'm still in awe of how such a thing as passion can be profited from.

The reason why God implants that insatiable appetite to do His will is because He saw a need to turn challenges into the food of champions. The only thing to keep people on their assignment is passion.

How do you explain why someone who's got a cracked voice from singing yesterday still holding the microphone and singing today? Only passion.

Passion is faith, patience, and perseverance combined. This is why the Bible said our testimony must be different: when others dare say that there's a casting down, we speak a different confession - we prophesy and insist that for us, it is a lifting up.

CONCLUSION

The process of gaining knowledge or understanding of your abilities, character, and feelings, begins with the knowledge of Jesus you have gained. When you gain the knowledge of Jesus, you equally gain the knowledge of yourself. This is what discovery is about and its benefits.

Now that you have read this book, you know by now that you're a reflection of God. You know you are here on Earth on an ambassadorial mission. You also know that you're not here on Earth for yourself, you belong to Someone and you represent that Person's will. This is why, though you have a will, you should allow your will to become sandwiched into His will. Also, you know you have tools that serve as the enablers you require to execute God's will and bring His counsel to the Earth. You are empowered to do this, and that is why you have potential.

Without the discovery of yourself and assignment, it will be difficult to walk a path of restoration of glory, of time, of power, of knowledge, of peace, of prosperity, and, of wholeness.

Discovery of self is key, without it, people will walk in darkness. Darkness excels in the absence of light. Think about the speed with which darkness runs out at the appearance of light, that's how everything grows back and comes back to you when you know the Christ, discover your unique self, and deploy your potential.

This is why this book has simplified and explained how important it is to be in the Vine so that your life can bear much fruits.

REFERENCES

Holden Stephen "Pop Briefs" *The New York Times.* Retrieved December 11, 2015.)

Dictionary.com

The Holy Bible, Amplified Version

Richard P. Fitzgibbons "Transsexual attractions and sexual reassignment surgery: Risks and potential risks" in National Library of Medicine, Linacre Q. November, 2015; 82(4): 337–350 https://www.ncbi.nlm.nih.gov/pmc/articles/PMC4771004/ accessed on 2 March, 2024.

Gender Dysphoria https://www.nhs.uk/conditions/gender-dysphoria/#:~:text=Gender%20dysphoria%20is%20a%20term,harmful%20impact%20on%20daily%20life

Kellen Baker and Arjee Restar, "Utilization and Costs of Gender-Affirming Care in a Commercially Insured Transgender Population" in THE JOURNAL OF LAW,

MEDICINE & ETHICS, 2022 Fall; 50(3): 456-470.

Laura Harold. "What is Dysfunctional Behavior in Families?" https://www.verywellmind.com/dysfunctional-defined-2610364 Accessed on 25 February, 2024.

Dr. Sean McDowell, "What does "Freedom" Means?" https://voices.lifeway.com/bible-theology/what-does-freedom-mean/#:~:text=After%20some%20discussion%20and%20reflection,law%20standing%20in%20their%20way Accessed on 24 February, 2024.

Aaron Delinger, "True Freedom vs. Unrestrained Choices," https://www.reformation21.org/blogs/true-freedom-vs-unrestrained-c.php Accessed on 25 February, 2024.

ABOUT THE BOOK

In this age where people are distracted from living life meaningfully because they are brainwashed into seeing and accepting a culture that detracts them from the very essence that brings fulfillment to living, as one that offers fun, fame, and fortune.

Life can be more.

If you were told that freedom and fulfillment are found in the things or activities that gratify the flesh, and you believed that lie, the reality should have, by now, told you otherwise. Every pursuit that hasn't satisfied your innermost core desire to express through freedom is a facade.

This is why this book offers a path to recovery. It doesn't matter how far ignorance has taken one, there's a plan and a path for recovery. It begins with discovery.

In this book, Emmanuel Ehigiator provides a blueprint for walking a life that counts - a life that offers true freedom and fulfillment.

ABOUT THE AUTHOR

Bishop Emmanuel Ehigiator is the founder of the Holy Ghost Deliverance Fire Ministry, with branches in Europe, Africa, and the United States where the Headquarters is situated in New York City. The Ministry is multifaceted, dealing with Healing, Deliverance, Life Coaching, and Counseling. His wife and partner in the ministry, Pastor Agnes Ehigiator, serves alongside him as senior Pastor of the New York branch.

Made in the USA
Middletown, DE
04 June 2024